j617.752 Stuart, Sandra Lee.
STU
    "Why do I have to
    wear glasses?"

$12.00

DATE			

③ July 96

BAKER & TAYLOR BOOKS

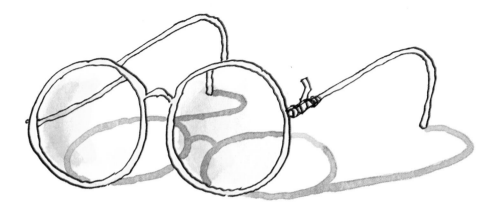

"WHY DO I HAVE TO WEAR GLASSES?"

By Sandra Lee Stuart

Illustrated by Arthur Robins

Library of Congress Cataloging-in-Publication Data

Stuart, Sandra Lee.
    Why do I have to wear glasses?

    "A Lyle Stuart book."
    Summary: Answers the title question, emphasizing
glasses are not punishment, but an ingenious solution
to a very common problem.
    1. Eyeglasses--Juvenile literature. 2. Vision--
Juvenile literature. [1. Eyeglasses. 2. Vision]
I. Robins, Arthur, ill. II. Title.
RE971.S78   1989   617.7'522   89-22156
ISBN 0-8184-0477-9

First Edition

Typesetting by Gryphon Typographers Inc.
Set in ITC Italia Book

Manufactured in the United States of America

A Lyle Stuart Book
Published by Carol Publishing Group
EDITORIAL OFFICES:
600 Madison Avenue
New York, New York 10022
SALES & DISTRIBUTION OFFICES:
120 Enterprise Avenue
Secaucus, New Jersey 07094

In Canada by Musson Book Company
A division of General Publishing Co. Limited
Don Mills, Ontario

To Aaron, with love and kisses

The acknowledgments:

A book such as this is a collaborative effort. Many thanks to the wonderful Arthur Robins for his zesty and wonderful illustrations, and to Steven Brower for his appealing design.

Thanks also to pediatric ophthalmologist, Dr. Leonard Nelson, of Wills Eye Hospital in Philadelphia, for his invaluable counsel and to Dr. Susan Gilman for her comments and suggestions.

We're going to talk about something extra special and very important.

You.

And your eyes.

Chances are things that you look at lately have been fuzzy or hard to see.

You might not have even known it.

Maybe your teacher noticed you were having trouble seeing things on the blackboard.

Or, maybe your Mom and Dad have wondered why you didn't see them waving to you from the other side of the park.

Or, it could be that your doctor noticed that one of your eyes was looking in the wrong direction.

It would be nice if there was a button or dial on your body like there is on a TV or VCR, a button that would get rid of the fuzzies and the wobblies and the can't-quite-see-it-rights. You could just fiddle with the button and zowie! Mickey Mouse doesn't have four ears anymore.

Too bad that's not what your belly button does.

That's the bad news.

The good news is there is something that will help you get rid of the fuzzies. It helps lots and lots of other people. Because—and this should be no surprise—you aren't the only person in the world who needs a little help with seeing. There are so many that you couldn't even count them if you tried.

This book is all about how wearing glasses will help you to see better.

People started to wear glasses a long time ago. It's an interesting story. Way back, mamas and papas and children and their dogs all lived in caves and didn't have television.

There was something else those cave-people didn't have. They didn't have eyeglasses. If someone didn't see well, it was just too bad.

There were many dangers for cave-people. It was no fun if they couldn't see them.

They might take longer steps than they thought they were taking, for one thing.

For another, people didn't jump in a car and go to the supermarket or McDonald's for food. Cavepeople had to hunt and anyone who couldn't see well ended up hungry.

"I'm home dear.
I just bashed a brontosaurus for dinner."

Not being able to see clearly was serious business even when the cave-people built little huts they call houses. And there was no way to help for a long time. Think of the problems there could have been if an ancient Egyptian who didn't see well had built the pyramids...

...or if knights in shining armor didn't know which way to point their lances...

...not to mention if William Tell wasn't sure where the apple was on his son's head...

Lucky thing some smart person came up with the idea of eyeglasses—they were called spectacles in the old days.

No one is really sure who made the first glasses. We do know that a long time ago the Chinese wore them.

In our part of the world it wasn't until about 700 years ago, in the 13th century, that a famous teacher and thinker named Roger Bacon started thinking about eyes and how they worked. Then he started thinking about how to help eyes that didn't see well and finally eyeglasses were invented.

(Want to hear something silly? At one time it was believed that only people who could read wore glasses. Not many people knew how to read in those days, and if you knew how, you were very important. So some people wore glasses even if they didn't need them because they wanted everyone to believe they could read.)

Roger Bacon wasn't the last person to work on seeing better. There were many people who came up with new ideas. Even Benjamin Franklin. When he wasn't flying kites in electrical storms and helping the United States to get started as a country, he was inventing glasses for people who had trouble seeing things far away and close up, just like himself.

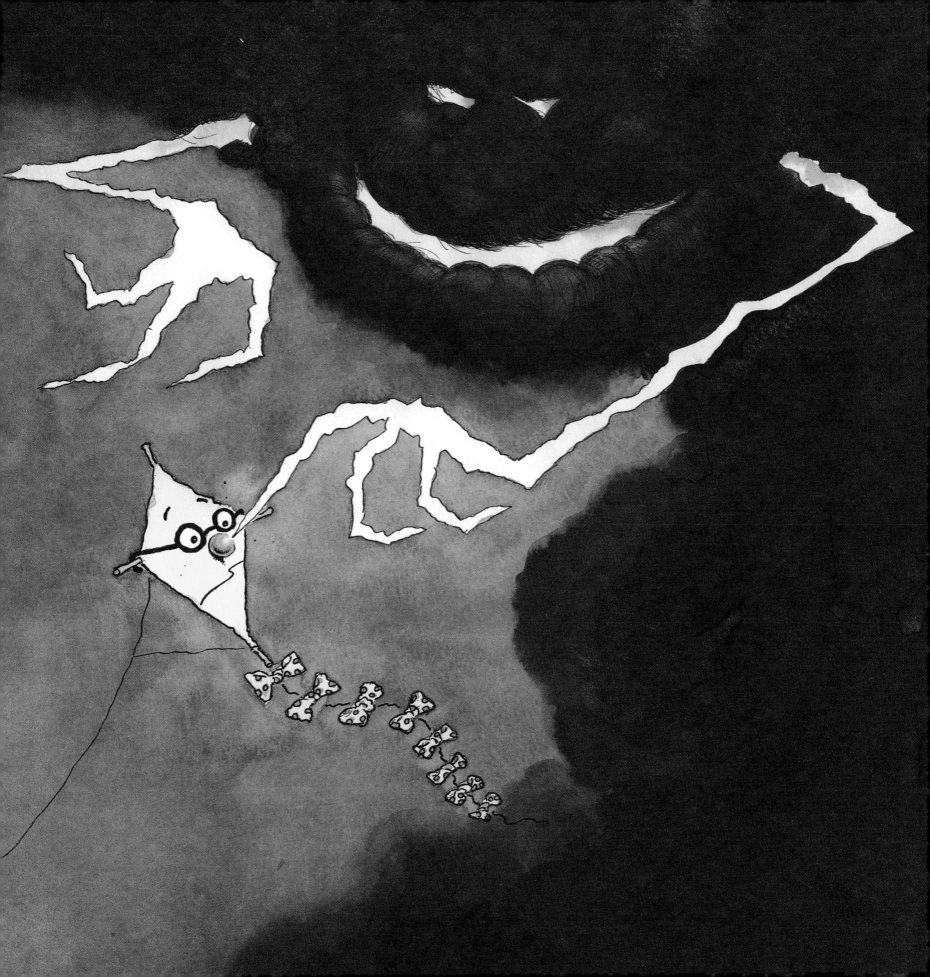

Okay, you're thinking, so glasses got invented. That's nice. But what about you? Why do you need them and not the kid next door? What is it about you that makes you need glasses?

To answer that, let's take a look at your eye. That's right. Get a mirror and look at your eye.

Now look at this picture of an eye.

They don't look much alike, do they? That's because in the mirror you're only seeing a little bit of your eye. There's a lot more to it.

The rest of your eye is mostly round—that's why it's called an "eyeball"—and it's tucked back in your head. A bunch of bones—the socket—protect it so it won't get bumped or hurt.

That's important because it would be easy to hurt your eye if it stuck out on your face like your nose. And you sure would look funny!

Let's start at the outside of the eye and work our way in. First there is the cornea (that's pronounced core-knee-ya). It's clear so light can go through it. It's strong to protect the rest of the eye.

Next is the iris (eye-ris). That has the color of your eye—brown, blue, green, gray, or whatever your color is.

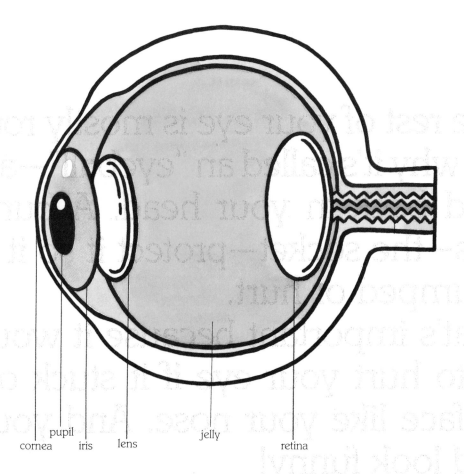

cornea pupil iris lens jelly retina

Right in the middle of the iris is the dark circle called the pupil. It's actually a little hole. When it's bright and there's a lot of light, the pupil gets smaller. When it's dark, it gets larger.

Next there's the lens. The lens can change shape, getting fatter or thinner, depending on how far away the thing you're looking at is. The lens puts things into focus.

Finally, at the back of the eye is a thin lining called the retina (reh-tin-ah). It's attached to the optic nerve. Optic means having to do with seeing. And a nerve carries messages to the brain. Like when you touch a hot pan. The nerve tells your brain it was hot and you yell "Yeoww!!!"

All these parts work together like a camera so that you can see. When you take a picture, you aim the camera, push the shutter to let light in, and the light falls onto the film. Your eye is not much different.

What keeps the eye round so it doesn't collapse like a balloon with no air is a clear jelly (not the kind you eat with peanut butter). It's mostly water.

Look out the window. Is it a bright sunny day? Suppose there's a black and white pussycat named Bruce sitting on a fence. The light rays that bounce off Bruce go through your cornea, pupil, the lens, and then are thrown back on the retina, which acts like the film or a picture screen. The only thing is that the picture of Bruce gets turned upside down at the lens so that when it reaches the retina the fence is on top and the cat below.

Don't worry, the optic nerve carries the message of "Bruce on a fence" to the brain. Your brain is very smart. It knows the pictures on the retina are upside down so it flip-flops the picture again, and, hooray, Bruce is right-side-up.

If you're wondering why you never noticed all these things happening when you look at something, that's because it happens faster than you can wink.

But everything has to be just right, every step of the way, if your brain is going to get a clear picture.

So what's wrong with your eyes, or more accurately, what's not just right?

There are many reasons why people don't see as well as they should.

Some people have trouble seeing things far away. Some people don't see things well that are close up. And for others, part of what they are looking at is blurry.

You probably want to know why.

It's usually because your eyeballs are slightly out of shape. We don't mean they're shaped like a starfish or camel, but they may be too long or too short. Or, it might not be your whole eyeball that's out of shape, only the cornea.

If you can't see the blackboard clearly when you're sitting in the back of the class, then you may be nearsighted. That means you see things better when they're near you.

That's called myopia. (My-oh-pee-ya. Boy, is your teacher going to be impressed with your pronunciation.)

If that's your problem, your eyeball is a teensy bit longer than it should be.

instead of this...

If you have myopia, a monkey up in a tree would look like this...

instead of this...

If you see things better when they are far away from you, you're what's called farsighted. Your eyes will get tired or what you're looking at will look a little blurry when you're reading a book. That's hypermetropia. (Do you really want to know how to pronounce that? Okay, it's a hi-purr-meh-troh-pee-ya, but we had to look that up in the dictionary. Good thing we were wearing our glasses.) That usually means the eyeball is too short.

Many young people under seven need glasses because they are farsighted.

If you are farsighted, a picture of Mother Goose in a nursery rhyme book would look like this...

instead of this...

If you have the blurries when you are looking at things both far away and close-up, then chances are you have an astigmatism (yikes! that's pronounced ah-stig-mah-tih-zum). It's caused by the cornea being not quite the right shape.

Then the beginning of a fairy story might look like this —

ONCE UPON A TIME...

instead of this — ONCE UPON A TIME...

Your eyes have to be the right shape and work together so your brain gets the correct message.

If the light that goes through the parts of your eyes doesn't get to your retina "screen" at the right angle, your brain will get the wrong message.

If your eye is a little out of shape, the light comes in at a different angle than it should and, poof, what you see gets bent out of shape as well.

You can breathe a sigh of relief and give a big "Thank You" that you're not living in the time when people lived in a cave. Because if your were, there wouldn't be anything you could do. You wouldn't see well and that would be that. Happily, there is a doctor who knows all about eyes and can find out what your eye problem is and help you. This doctor is called an ophthalmologist (ahf-thal-mah-low-jist).

The doctor will do several things when examining your eyes. Drops of a liquid will be put in your eyes. The doctor will look at them with an instrument that looks like a little flashlight, and show you some pictures or letters and ask you what they are. The doctor even has machines to measure the shape of your eyes. All you have to do is say what you see.

It's that simple.

The doctor will figure out the problem, and then decide what to do about it. Sometimes that means wearing glasses. The doctor has machines for telling exactly which glasses are right for you.

Glasses can make the light come into your eyes and up to your brain the way it should.

Have you been wondering why you need to wear glasses and your friend may not?

Let's talk about some things that you may be wondering about.

Did you hang upside down too long on the monkey bars?

Did you make silly faces at your pesty baby sitters?

Did you tell a lie?

Did you sit too close to the television?

Did you forget to eat your carrots?

Nope. It wasn't because you did anything bad or you forgot to do something good. Nope. It's simply that just like a short person needs a ladder to reach a high step—you need glasses to help you to see better. That's okay. Everyone needs help sometimes.

Superman needs Lois Lane to get rid of any Kryptonite that might get too close to him.

Airline pilots need directions from the control tower to help them land.

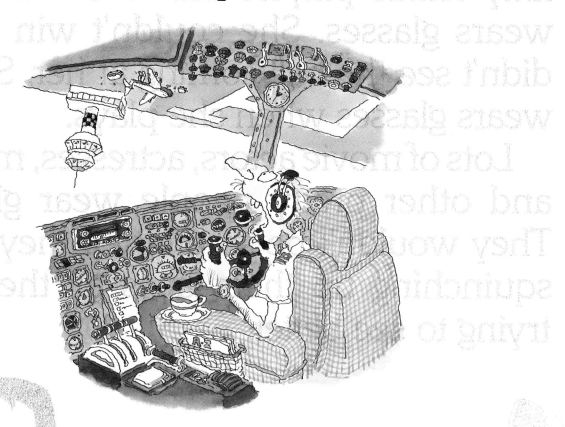

Moms and Dads need maps to find new parks.

And lots of people need help to see better. You're one of them.

Some very talented people wear glasses.

New York Yankee slugger Reggie Jackson wore glasses when he hit three home runs in the 1978 World Series. He had to see the ball to hit it.

Martina Navratilova, one of the greatest lady tennis players that ever has lived, wears glasses. She couldn't win if she didn't see the ball coming at her. So she wears glasses when she plays.

Lots of movie actors, actresses, models and other pretty people wear glasses. They wouldn't be so pretty if they were squinching up their faces all the time trying to see better.

Lots of other famous people have worn glasses. Presidents like Abraham Lincoln. Scientists like Albert Einstein. Muppet babies like Squeeter.

Remember. You want to be the best you can be and do the best you can. And your eyes may need a little help. That's what glasses are for.

Will you have to wear them all your life? It's hard to say. Everyone is different. But if you do, that's okay.

With glasses, you'll be able to:

Recognize your best friend way down the block.

See a movie without having to sit in the front row where your neck gets stiff from looking straight up.

Catch a ball better.

Thread a needle on the first try,
or at least the second.

Take better pictures — because you can't focus a camera
if your eyes are out of focus.

Read your comic book easier.

And best of all, when you look in the mirror, you'll finally be able to see what you really look like. Great.

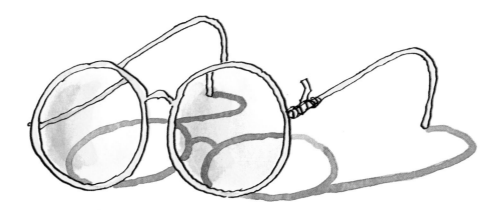